anythink

D0793202

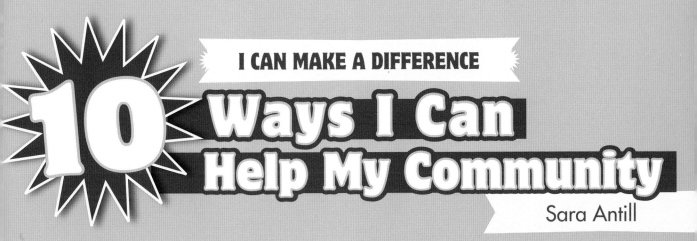

I CAN MAKE A DIFFERENCE

10 Ways I Can Help My Community

Sara Antill

PowerKiDS press.

New York

Published in 2012 by The Rosen Publishing Group, Inc.
29 East 21st Street, New York, NY 10010

First Edition

Editor: Jennifer Way
Book Design: Ashley Drago

Photo Credits: Cover Jupiterimages/Pixland/Thinkstock; pp. 4–5, 13 Jupiterimages/Brand X Pictures/Thinkstock; pp. 6–7 Leland Bobbe/Getty Images; p. 8 Jupiterimages/Creatas/Thinkstock; p. 9 © Jim West/age fotostock; p. 10 David McNew/Getty Images; p. 11 Corey Sipkin/NY Daily News Archive via Getty Images; p. 12 Doug Pensinger/Getty Images; pp. 14–15 Thinkstock Images/Getty Images; p. 16 © www.iStockphoto.com/DenGuy; p. 17 © www.iStockphoto.com/Kali9; p. 18 © www.iStockphoto.com/Nic Neufeld; p. 19 Littleny/Shutterstock.com; pp. 20–21 Jung Yeon-Je/AFP/Getty Images; p. 22 © www.iStockphoto.com/Jani Bryson.

Library of Congress Cataloging-in-Publication Data

Antill, Sara.
  10 ways I can help my community / by Sara Antill. — 1st ed.
      p. cm. — (I can make a difference)
  Includes index.
  ISBN 978-1-4488-6202-3 (library binding) — ISBN 978-1-4488-6363-1 (pbk.) —
  ISBN 978-1-4488-6364-8 (6-pack)
  1. Vocational guidance—Juvenile literature. 2. Social participation—Juvenile literature. 3. Occupations—Juvenile literature. 4. Professions—Juvenile literature. I. Title. II. Title: Ten ways I can help my community.
  HF5381.2.A58 2012
  361.7'4—dc23
                                             2011019503

Manufactured in the United States of America

CPSIA Compliance Information: Batch #WW12PK: For Further Information contact Rosen Publishing, New York, New York at 1-800-237-9932

Contents

Help Your Community

You can probably think of many times that you have helped someone in your family or a friend. Did you know, though, that there are ways that you can help hundreds or even thousands of people at once?

This book will show you 10 fun, simple ways that you can help your **community**. A community is a group of people who live and work together in a certain place. Some of the activities in this book can be done on your own. However, many of them will be more fun if you share them with your friends and family!

Many schools and community groups have food drives. Collecting canned goods for a food drive is one way you can help your community.

1 Keep a Park Beautiful

A local park is an important part of any community. However, when a park has lots of trash, or **litter**, on the ground, people may not want to spend time there. One way that you can help your community is by picking

up litter on the ground and putting it in a trash can. You can also make signs asking other people to do the same!

You can keep your park beautiful by planting trees. Trees help make the air that we breathe cleaner. See if any groups in your community are planning to plant trees on Earth Day.

Picking up litter as a group activity will make your local park nicer for everyone.

2 Donate Food

Not everyone in a community has enough to eat. Some families have very little money to buy food. You can help by **donating** food to a **food drive**. Many food drives ask for people to donate canned food, such as vegetables. This is because canned food lasts for a long time without going bad.

Your school may have a food drive for your community. There are also national groups that work to get food donations to communities, such as Feeding America.

3 Volunteer in a Soup Kitchen

Soup kitchens are places that serve hot meals to people who are hungry. **Charity** groups or religious groups often run them. Soup kitchens serve more than just soup, though. You and your family can **volunteer** to help cook the meal, serve it, or even clean up.

There are lots of different jobs for volunteers in a soup kitchen. Meals need to be prepared and served, which means there is something volunteers of any age can do.

9

4 Donate to a Toy Drive

Some families may not be able to buy their children gifts such as new toys. You can make another child happy by donating to a toy drive. You and your parents can pick out a toy to buy in a store. You can also donate some of your toys that you do not use anymore. Just remember to donate only toys that are new or gently used.

When you donate to a toy drive, you can find out if the charity has a wish list of toys. This helps them have toys for kids of different ages.

5 Donate to a Coat Drive

Do you live in a place that gets cold in the winter? Some people cannot afford to replace worn-out coats or coats that have become too small. You can help by donating a new or gently used coat to a coat drive.

If your community does not have a coat drive, you can help get one started! One Warm Coat is a national group that helps communities organize coat drives.

6 Send a Care Package

First Lady Michelle Obama (left) helped kid volunteers put together care packages for soldiers in Iraq and Afghanistan.

Is anyone in your family in the **military**? There are about 1.4 million men and women serving in the US military today. Many of them serve overseas for months or years at a time. There may be people from your community serving overseas right now.

When you are putting together a care package, you can also write a short letter. A personal letter is a thoughtful touch that will make the soldier feel appreciated.

It can be hard for a **soldier** to be away from home for so long. You can help him or her by sending a **care package**. A care package can include sunscreen, toothpaste, or a tasty treat! Small things can mean a lot to a soldier. Best of all, care packages remind these soldiers that people are thinking about them!

7 Visit a Nursing Home

Do your grandparents live near you? Some grandparents live in **nursing homes**. These are places for people who need special, long-term care. Often older, or **elderly**, people live there when they are no longer

able to take care of all of their own needs.

Many people in nursing homes do not have family nearby to come and visit them. You can make a big difference in someone's day by visiting a nursing home. You can sit quietly and talk, play a board game, or put on a performance with some friends or a group from school.

Spending one-on-one time with a person who is in a nursing home will brighten that person's day.

8 Volunteer at an Animal Shelter

The Humane Society and the ASPCA are two national groups that help animals. They sometimes have adoption drives. Both groups are good sources for learning about helping animals.

Someone who loves animals might enjoy volunteering at an animal shelter. Call your local chapter of the Humane Society or the American Society for the Prevention of Cruelty to Animals (ASPCA) to see if they have a junior volunteer program. Young people can often volunteer if their parents volunteer with them.

Volunteers might walk dogs, feed cats, or help others learn about pet **adoption**. You could also ask your parents if your family can **foster** a pet while it is waiting to be adopted. This can be a good way to learn about pet adoption and responsible pet ownership.

Your parents may let you foster a shelter animal. It is a big responsibility, but it can be very rewarding.

This family is walking together in the Susan G. Komen Race for the Cure. This is a charity run and walk that raises money for breast cancer research.

It may seem simple, but you can help people in your community and the world just by walking! Every year millions of people join in charity walks. Walkers agree to walk for a certain amount of time or a certain distance. To support them, people donate money to a charity.

There are charity walks to raise money for many different illnesses, such as cancer, AIDS, and cystic fibrosis. The American Cancer Society's Relay for Life raised more than $1.2 billion between 2008 and 2010. One out of every four walkers in the Relay for Life is younger than 18!

When you walk for charity, you can make it even more fun by making T-shirts or signs for your group. This girl is taking part in a walk for the American Liver Foundation.

It can seem like a lot of work to help your community on your own. Why not join a group that is already working to change things for the better? Groups like the United Way, Boy Scouts of America and Girl Scouts of the USA, and generationOn have service

events all year that you can join. These events can include cleaning up a beach, helping younger children with their homework, or planting a community garden.

By volunteering with a group, you can often make a big difference in a short time. You can also meet new friends who care as much about their communities as you do!

The Boy Scouts and the Girls Scouts are two groups for kids that do lots of community volunteering. The Web link on page 24 will take you to a list of these and all the other organizations mentioned in this book.

Spread the News

One of the most important ways that you can help your community is by getting other people excited about helping as well! Tell your class about the different ways that you have found to help. You can even talk to a teacher about starting a chapter of the Kids Care Club in your school. The Kids Care Club is a youth volunteer group that helps kids organize community service activities.

You can help your community each day in big and small ways. The ideas in this book are just the beginning. What other ways can you think of to help your community?

You can form a community service group with your classmates. Planting flowers and trees is an activity that your group can organize.

Glossary

adoption (uh-DOP-shun) Taking an animal into your home to become your pet.

care package (KER PA-kij) A package sent as a gift.

charity (CHER-uh-tee) A group that gives help to the needy.

community (kuh-MYOO-nih-tee) A place where people live and work together or the people who make up such a place.

donating (DOH-nayt-ing) Giving something away.

elderly (EL-der-lee) Older than middle age.

food drive (FOOD DRYV) When people collect food for donation.

foster (FOS-tur) To care for as part of one's family.

litter (LIH-ter) Trash that is thrown on the ground instead of being placed in a bag or a trash can.

military (MIH-luh-ter-ee) The part of the government, such as the army or navy, that keeps its citizens safe.

nursing homes (NURS-ing HOHMZ) Places for people who need special, long-term care.

soldier (SOHL-jur) Someone who is in an army.

soup kitchens (SOOP KIH-chenz) Places where needy people can get meals to eat.

volunteer (vah-lun-TEER) To give one's time without pay.

Index

Web Sites

Due to the changing nature of Internet links, PowerKids Press has developed an online list of Web sites related to the subject of this book. This site is updated regularly. Please use this link to access the list: www.powerkidslinks.com/diff/commun/